MASTERING THE INTERVIEW

UNLOCKING SUCCESS THROUGH EXPERT INTERVIEW STRATEGIES

STARLIGHT INYAMA

DEDICATION

This work is dedicated to God Almighty, for His mercies and goodness.

TABLE OF CONTENTS

Chapter 1

THE ULTIMATE GUIDE TO JOB INTERVIEWS

The Foundation

To excel in job interviews, start with thorough planning. Before stepping into the interview room, conduct comprehensive research on the company and the role you're seeking. This showcases your genuine interest and helps you align your qualities with their requirements.

Practice is essential. Prepare answers for common interview questions, focusing on how you can effectively highlight your skills and attributes. Incorporate anecdotes from your past experiences that can be relevant in various contexts. This not only adds authenticity to your responses but also boosts your confidence.

When it comes to the actual interview, first impressions matter. Arrive punctually, dress appropriately, and carry copies of your resume and necessary documents.

Remember, a smile speaks volumes! Throughout the interview, remain true to yourself. Avoid pretending to be someone you're not. Don't hesitate to ask questions or provide examples that back your statements. Honesty is key, as your potential employer wants to understand your genuine self.

Lastly, after the interview, don't hesitate to follow up. Sending a brief email or letter expressing gratitude can leave a positive impact and reinforce your interest in the position.

Mirroring Technique

This technique involves more than just mimicking the foyer's painting. Instead, it's about adopting a similar tone and demeanor to your interviewer. By subtly aligning yourself with their mannerisms, you can convey a sense of rapport and comfort.

This approach is less awkward than a secret handshake and serves as a discreet way to establish a connection. It signals to the interviewer that you're in sync and creates a positive subconscious impact. Also known as "matching and mirroring," this tactic increases the likelihood of the interviewer feeling a connection with you.

However, it's important to use this technique subtly, avoiding overt or confrontational imitation. Observe your interviewer's posture and tone, and mirror them discreetly to make a lasting positive impression.

Persuasive Approach to Addressing Flaws in an Interview

When asked about your flaws, take a unique and impactful approach that sets you apart.

Instead of a generic response, consider turning the conversation on its head. Playfully admit that you struggle with interviews. This unexpected and courageous answer showcases your self-awareness and adds a touch of humor to the dialogue.

This method has a few important benefits. It doesn't just make things more relaxed and reduce stress, but it also highlights that an interview is a two-way conversation. Adding some humor makes everyone feel at ease and more involved.

But here's where the strategy truly shines: By presenting interview performance as a weakness and then discussing how you've worked to overcome it, you create a strong impression.

Subconsciously, the interviewer is likely to think, "If they manage their weaknesses effectively, imagine the strength they bring!"

Incorporating this approach not only showcases your authenticity and adaptability but also demonstrates your potential for growth and improvement. So, embrace your flaws with humor, turn them into a narrative of personal development, and leave a lasting positive impact on your interviewer.

"Speaking with Authority in Interviews"

During interviews, it's easy to fall into the trap of rambling on, but here's a crucial tip: Know when to stop talking.

Interviewers appreciate your ability to articulate your thoughts confidently and succinctly. Maintain focus, speak with assurance, and don't shy away from pauses to gather your thoughts. Opt for a moment of silence over speaking in circles or relying on filler words like "um" or "like."

Confidence is key. Even if you make a few mistakes, a self-assured demeanor can make a positive impression on the interviewer.

Summing it up:
Remember, at its core, every interview question boils down to whether you can contribute to their profits or decrease their costs.

And it's wise to position yourself in the latter category. This doesn't mean embellishing or lying, but rather presenting yourself in a way that highlights your potential value to them.

Craft each response to emphasize how you will be an asset rather than an expense.

Illustration: Take the common question about a time you failed. Avoid discussing a complete failure or acting infallible. Instead, share a real-life example where things went wrong but were ultimately rectified. For instance, discuss a Project X setback that led to a valuable discovery or the resolution of an issue, ultimately contributing to future successes.

Closing an Interview with Impact

To leave a strong final impression in an interview, consider this effective strategy: inquire if the interviewer has any concerns regarding your application, resume, or interview responses.

While it may be seen as bold, this approach showcases your confidence and proactive attitude. It also grants you the opportunity to address potential issues directly.

Be confident that this approach has a proven track record of success. It's a great method to reveal any points you may not have explained thoroughly or that could have been misinterpreted.

This approach could even allow you to alleviate any reservations and solidify your candidacy. This simple step could be the determining factor in securing the job offer.

Chapter 2

TIPS FOR SUCCESS IN BEHAVIORAL INTERVIEWS

Last autumn, I started actively looking for a summer internship. Despite having the required technical skills, I faced difficulty in effectively presenting them during interviews. Here, I'll share strategies I've discovered for excelling in behavioral interviews, especially from the viewpoint of a college student.

1. Display Confidence: Imagine impressing a stranger or making a friend. Interviews are similar but more stressful. Projecting ease and confidence improves the interviewer's perception of you. Dressing in something you love boosts confidence, and self-care enhances your overall demeanor.

2. "Tell Me About Yourself": Respond by sharing your background, education, relevant experience, interests, and reasons for applying. Initiate this discussion rather than waiting for questions. It creates a natural flow and helps you highlight your successes early on.

3. Prepare Your Resume: Each detail on your resume should have a compelling story. Be ready to discuss any bullet point in depth and relate it to your potential contributions to the company.

4. Recall Relevant Stories: Expect common behavioral questions like conflicts with coworkers or challenging projects. Share experiences particular to your background, avoiding negativity and emphasizing lessons learned.

5. Embrace Humility: Avoid overt self-promotion. Instead, exhibit your qualities through your behavior, communication, and descriptions of your experiences. Show why you're the ideal candidate without explicitly stating it.

In conclusion, behavioral interviews can be as challenging as technical ones. With preparation, perseverance, support, and belief in yourself, you can excel and even find enjoyment in the process.

Chapter 3

HOW TO APPROACH JOB INTERVIEW PREPARATION WITH MINDFULNESS

The challenge lies in understanding the role's compatibility with your aspirations and whether it aligns with your desired path for the next three years. It's important to recognize that the interviewer might already have an ideal candidate in mind.

However, this doesn't mean the outcome is predetermined or that there's no hope. Keep in mind that the interviewer is a person with diverse experiences. It's your responsibility during the interview to assess whether both you and the interviewer possess the qualities that would make the upcoming years of full-time work enjoyable, considering you'll be spending 8 hours a day, five days a week together.

Considering that you'll likely spend more time with your boss than with your romantic partner, ensuring a thorough interview with your potential boss is crucial.

Effective Interview Preparation: Proven Strategies You Can Implement

1. Clearly define your desired outcome for the interview. Approach the interview with a clear understanding of its purpose, whether it's for information gathering, practice, or potential employment. Not expressing your intent might lead to confusion and reduced confidence.

2. Research the company and its structure. Gain insight into the company's culture,

products, organizational setup, and financial status. This knowledge helps you understand decision-making processes and overall dynamics.

3. Learn about your interviewer online. Utilize platforms like LinkedIn, Twitter, or Facebook to learn about your interviewer's personality and background, giving you a better sense of who they are.

4. Familiarize yourself with the company's products. If you're interested in working for the company, it's important to appreciate and understand its products. Your enthusiasm should align with what the company offers.

5. Seek advice from network contacts. Connect with people who have experience in the position through platforms like LinkedIn to gain insights and perspectives.

6. Prepare for interview questions. Expect technical or role-specific questions based on the position. Be ready to showcase your skills and proficiency.

7. Keep your self-introduction brief. Since the interviewer has already seen your resume, a concise introduction is sufficient. This sets the stage for more in-depth discussions.

8. Address the opening question thoughtfully. After your introduction, allow a brief pause for the interviewer to start the conversation. If they don't, you can inquire about the most crucial aspects of the job, demonstrating your interest in their priorities. This can lead to meaningful discussions about your potential role.

9. Ensure your answers include instances that showcase both your strengths and areas for improvement. Research indicates that people learn best through stories, and this

applies to interviewers too. Incorporating memorable anecdotes into your responses helps the interviewer recall your answers.

It's wise to prepare multiple stories for common questions, highlighting a skill you possess and an area where you aim to grow.

This approach aligns with the appeal of reality shows where personal development is captivating, a quality your potential employer will appreciate. Authenticity matters; fabricating stories can easily be exposed in today's interconnected world.

10. Identifying your stakeholders and supervisors is crucial. While many inquire about their managers, stakeholders within a large organization hold significant importance. Familiarizing yourself with stakeholders related to your role is a prudent move. These individuals might even wield more influence than your immediate manager. Observe how your manager

discusses them; this sheds light on the dynamics at play.

11. Look at details about the company culture with a questioning mindset. Because everyone's unique life experiences shape their views, getting an exact picture of the company culture is uncommon.

12. Your voice matters in phone interviews Even though video interviews have become more common, phone interviews still have a role in the hiring process. Short phone interviews help hiring managers evaluate candidates effectively. The tone of your voice and the words you choose greatly influence a successful phone interview.

13. Having a good internet connection is important for Skype or Zoom interviews Video interviews are now frequent in the time after COVID-19, making remote work easier. Although video quality is usually fine,

make sure your software and internet are dependable. A weak connection might disrupt communication and unintentionally indicate a lack of tech skills.

14. Should You Send Post-Interview Follow-Up Emails?

Some people recommend sending follow-up emails after interviews to remind the hiring manager of your interest and leave a positive impression. However, this might not always be necessary, as managers are often eager to fill positions quickly. There are exceptions in fields like sales, where proactive follow-up is appreciated. Sending a follow-up email can be valuable if you have extra materials or relevant articles to share, showcasing your dedication.

15. Handling assignments after interviews

Assignments can be beneficial and stressful for interviewees. Approach them with your best effort and utilize the opportunity to gain insights into the role. The assignment also offers hiring managers a glimpse into your thinking process. On the flip side, you might realize the role isn't the right fit or the manager could discern a misalignment.

Chapter 4

THE SECRET MINDSET TO MASTERING INTERVIEWS

The hidden perspective for excelling in interviews is outlined below:

1. Cultivate Mental Resilience for Stress and Anxiety

Even the most self-assured individuals can grapple with worry and tension before stepping into a job interview. In today's uncertain job market, securing employment is more challenging than in the recent past. This situation adds an extra layer of complexity to the interview process.

2. Mastering Interview Anxiety: The Key Approach

You're not alone in experiencing pre-interview anxiety—virtually everyone does. The challenge lies in preventing anxiety from overwhelming your capabilities.

To bolster your confidence and effectively manage interview-related stress, adopt the following strategies. By incorporating these steps, you'll be better prepared to navigate the recruitment process.

Remember, as you delve into company research and familiarize yourself with the interviewers, your anxiety will naturally decrease. Practicing your elevator pitch and aligning your skills with the job requirements are also crucial steps.

As a result, instead of feeling anxious, you'll exude positivity, confidence, and control. The anticipation of entering the interview room or joining a video conference will transform from dread to excitement.

Your upbeat energy won't go unnoticed by hiring managers and interviewers. They'll appreciate your thorough understanding of the role, and your organized, driven, and passionate demeanor will make a strong impression.

3. What to Expect During the Hiring Journey

Feeling apprehensive during the hiring process is completely normal. Facing a barrage of questions from unfamiliar faces and undergoing constant evaluation is a daunting experience.

Throughout the interview, every nuance of your body language, facial expressions, and even your attire is under scrutiny. The process often involves enduring a series of interviews, ranging from a handful to even ten sessions, spanning three to six months or more.

If the intensity of the procedure isn't enough, many companies also fall short when it comes to providing constructive feedback or guidance. There can be prolonged gaps in communication between the company and candidates, leaving you feeling adrift and unsupported.

4. Mastering Nerves and Building Confidence Successfully

The groundwork you lay in the pre-interview phase significantly influences positive outcomes. One key to success is immersing yourself in comprehensive knowledge about the company, its team, its mission, and the products or services it offers.

Delve into the LinkedIn profiles of those who will interview you. You can view profiles discreetly. Analyze their job roles, tenure, previous employers, and educational background. This intel serves as conversational ammunition, helping you initiate dialogue and establish common ground.

Thoroughly read the job description. Ensure your resume aligns with the requirements. Craft a pitch that highlights how you can acquire the skills or leverage existing expertise to fulfill responsibilities if you lack certain qualifications.

Gather insider insights. Identify connections within the company. If you lack direct contacts, tap into your network to find someone who can offer insights. Gaining insider perspectives on the organization and specific roles can be immensely valuable. If working with a recruiter, leverage their knowledge. Ask for insights into the company, interviewers, hiring manager, and organizational culture.

Research online to uncover recent positive or negative changes within the company.

Craft a concise elevator pitch. This is akin to a TV commercial. Your self-promotion should take under a minute. The phrase's origin lies in the concept of grabbing someone's attention during a brief elevator ride.

Your pitch should be succinct, and clear, and showcase how you possess nearly all the essential qualifications for the role. Practice your elevator pitch aloud with others. While it might sound perfect in your mind, saying it aloud will reveal any necessary adjustments.

Remember, your initial rendition might need refinement, even if it seems flawless in your head.

5. Smooth Out All the Details

Plan to navigate the logistics seamlessly. For face-to-face interviews, be aware of the interview location and estimated travel time. It's a good idea to have extra copies of your CV on hand, as there might be additional interviewers added at the last minute.

Arriving early offers a chance for a stroll around the area, easing nerves and sparking conversations. Grab mints to engage with security and staff upon entering the building, fostering a sense of ease.

Consume food and drink to prevent hunger and tiredness. Take a moment to freshen up and check your appearance before the interview. Have a mint to freshen your breath before going into the interview room.

For online interviews, it's important to evaluate sound, lighting, backdrop, and internet connection. Confirm you're using the correct platform and have the right credentials. Also, gather contact info for the interview lead in case of issues. By addressing these factors, you'll be prepared for a seamless and confident interview.

6. "I Will Secure That Job"

Before your in-person or video interview, take a moment for a few deep breaths. Inhale for four counts, pause briefly and exhale for four counts. You'll find this technique wonderfully effective for relaxation and mental clarity.

Embrace self-talk: Reflect on your qualifications, and your drive for the role, and visualize your previous successes.

Remind yourself: "I am the ideal candidate for this role. I deserve it, and I am capable of achieving it." Rest assured, you have what it takes to secure that job.

Chapter 5

REASONS FOR INTERVIEW FAILURES

Many individuals often express frustration over their unsuccessful interview attempts, uncertain about the possibility of change.

Rest assured, change is possible, and I will share comprehensive insights within this book.

The Culprit Isn't Your Resume if Interview Success Eludes You

Numerous job seekers believe that their lack of interview success stems from inadequate experience matching their resume.

However, this isn't always the case.

Employers wouldn't invite you for an interview if they weren't interested in your CV.

Once you're in the interview, the responsibility shifts to you to leave a positive impression. This encompasses how you present your background, your demeanor, the inquiries you pose, and various other elements.

Your resume's primary goal is to secure you an interview, and if it accomplishes that, it serves its purpose.

Once you're in the interview, it's up to you to make an impression. This includes how you convey your experience, your demeanor, the questions you ask them at the conclusion, and other factors.

Common Reasons Why People Fail Job Interviews:

1. Inadequate research on the job and company: Neglecting research can leave a negative impression on employers. Thoroughly understanding the job responsibilities and company details is crucial.

2. Lack of proactive questions: Failing to ask insightful questions can show disinterest. Engaging in meaningful conversations about the role and company demonstrates your commitment.

3. Omitting post-interview thank-you emails: Sending thank-you emails after the interview shows professionalism and dedication to going the extra mile.

4. Providing inconsistent or dishonest information: Honesty is essential. Being open about areas where you lack knowledge

or experience is better than trying to deceive.

5. Unclear career goals: Employers appreciate candidates who know what they want. Showing a clear direction in your career goals helps build confidence in your commitment.

6. Not justifying interest in the specific position: Linking your skills and aspirations to the job's responsibilities and the company's values is crucial.

7. Lack of enthusiasm: Demonstrating enthusiasm and excitement about the role can positively impact the interviewer's perception of your fit for the position.

8. Being too modest: While remaining humble is important, confidently discussing your achievements and skills showcases your potential value to the company.

9. Focusing on yourself, not the company: Show how your abilities align with the company's needs. Tailoring your responses to emphasize what you can bring to them is key.

10. Unwillingness to adapt: Being flexible and open to new ideas is vital. Employers want candidates who can integrate into their company culture.

11. Poor demeanor or appearance: A professional appearance and positive demeanor are essential for creating a strong initial impression.

12. Not building a personal connection: Establishing rapport with the interviewer helps you stand out as a potential team member, rather than just another candidate.

13. Mismatched skills: Sometimes, the skills you offer may not align with the company's

needs. While this can be a factor, focus on improving what you can control.

Remember, while there are elements outside your control, you can take steps to improve your interview performance and increase your chances of success.